(Notes fro

the word prisoner hau

it denies my existence as a man.
likewise do my living conditions.

My sanity is hidden somewhere
within the code 251534. More
important than my name, it
has tried to become me.

    humanity: a ghost that finds no
    refuge in my mind
    time has become my nemesis
    depression my constant companion

And yet i am more than i was
fighting with my soul
to do more than survive
i will not settle for survival

my family supports me.
without my family who would i be?

in slow steps i walk
    making sure to inhale

Third World Press

TWP

P.O. Box 19730
7822 South Dobson
Chicago, Illinois 60619

Progressive Black
Publishing Since 1967

Reginald Betts #251534
Sussex 1 State Prison
24414 Musselwhite
Waverly, VA 23891

Doggerel

Also by
Reginald Dwayne Betts

POETRY
Shahid Reads His Own Palm
Bastards of the Reagan Era
Felon
Redaction (with Titus Kaphar)

MEMOIR
A Question of Freedom

W. W. Norton & Company
Independent Publishers Since 1923

Reginald Dwayne Betts

Doggerel

Poems

/ˈdɒg(ə)rəl/ *n*

DAW-guh-ruhl

1   ~~of verse: comic, burlesque, and usually composed in irregular rhythm. Also: (of verse or writing) badly composed or expressed; trivial.~~

2   nah, just a Black man writing poems about his dog, & all the dogs he encounters on the street, & how having an extra four feet changed his world, & then he falls in love.

For information about permission to reproduce
selections from this book, write to
Permissions, W. W. Norton & Company, Inc.,
500 Fifth Avenue, New York, NY 10110

For information about special discounts for bulk purchases,
please contact W. W. Norton Special Sales at
specialsales@wwnorton.com or 800-233-4830

Manufacturing by Versa Press
Book design by Practise
Production manager: Louise Mattarelliano

ISBN 978-1-324-08925-4
       978-1-324-10616-6 (pbk.)

W. W. Norton & Company, Inc.
500 Fifth Avenue, New York, N.Y. 10110
www.wwnorton.com

W. W. Norton & Company Ltd.
15 Carlisle Street, London W1D 3BS

1 2 3 4 5 6 7 8 9 0

for Lori, for Can

Doggerel

This Future

Was it lost to that red mower's spell—his future?
A symbol? Purpling bruise nor past foretell his future.

Things we carry: hiccups & regrets, lost receipts,
The shrapnel of my mind—all death knell his future?

Dear Father, how you forget what I remember?
Your son's nightmares threaten to quell his future.

& still, why not forgiveness or mercy, g–d asks,
What makes him sacrifice his soul? Motel his future?

Everything they say is wrong about his suffering,
Earned or not, it prolly ain't only Orwell his future.

His father alive; his mother been dead.
& all them Black stories, they won't sell his future.

"I never said most of the things I said," says the catcher;
Yogi's namesake barks, no bounds, to smell his future.

My son, my son—you don't know the thing 'round my neck;
Dear Albatross, tell father a crackpipe bells his future.

I'm afraid when I look to the right, my brother vanishes,
As if he never exists; no, exists less. This cell: his future.

Everyone here is me, all of us chasing love, or hope,
Or the gospel, or however this madman retells his future.

His bruja—wild in a way, Can confesses: here is fertile;
As in they go together. She & Shy foretell this future.

On Joy

for Debby

You ask me how I'm doing
& I realize there are not enough
Words for joy in this language,
Not like in German, where a man
Can whisper a phrase for relief
That roughly translates to
It felt like a stone falling from
My heart. The g–ds must not
Know the things I've wanted in this
World. In prison, a letter is called
A kite, as if words alone can gift
A man wings. & I want to tell
You that my body is a kite
Swept into the wind, to say some
Days my heart is the wildest
Hungriest thing I know.
Whatever about choices.
Follow me now, the erratic thing
That knocks against my rib cage
Says. & I have, everywhere,
Off cliffs in cities whose names
I cannot pronounce, back into
Prisons, to walking Alec in a park
With Debby, to my sons' basketball

Games, to weeping & to down on
My knees, to something I've
Never actually called joy, but
Just might be, that remembering
Of all the things I believed needed
Letting go, only to learn
The raft on which I ride into
My todays was built with them.

Losing Weight

When I wanted to lose weight,
When I started, it began with hunger;
With needing to feel my body
Asking for more, of it all, butter & salt
& forgiveness for Hennessy cursing
Through these veins, another tide
Ushering me back to all my prisons.
It started with fear. Or not fear, but
Walking, literally, with what I'd feared:
A dog with teeth that flared when
Threatened, even if them vampire fangs
Wouldn't break my skin if I were another
Treat. We'd walk to the driveway's end,
Then more steps until the space
Past the yard felt safe; until this Jack
Russell Terrier that fit inside my palm
As a pistol once did, let me slip all
Those memories. & yes, I began
Wanting the world as she did, full gulps
Of its scent until my nose twitched
Like a conduit for what might be
Possible. & somehow more & more
& more of me disappeared, during
Those moments with my loves,

The puppy leading & the two lights
Illuminating my world, & maybe it's folly
For a man to admit he is in love with
A son young enough to still believe
His father's burdens will not touch him,
& an older son who knows it doesn't
Matter, because the only burden too
Worrying is never seeing your father
Weep. & now entire pieces of who I was
Have begun to fall from my body,
Worries & so much more, as I become,
Wildly, as light as wind, as when my only
Burden was the cells I left behind.

Will They Reminisce Over You

My father's name is the first I know.
To say his nom de guerre is to summon
A map of woe. For me, this man who drops
Discursive in casual conversation is never
A crackhead; instead, substrate & stratosphere;
A concordance of mistakes; the tapestry
I lift from my shoulders & walk into the world.

Race

Once, up 92 if a single step, I raced
Taylor, a small Jack Russell whose heart,
When resting, beats 50 times per minute,
& mine beats 53, if at all, low—low
Like the resting rate of the Champ
The year he quit being Cassius Clay,
& chose to become Muhammad Ali,
& ain't we all out here trying to become
Somebody. So once, when puppy wanted
Me to release her leash, instead, of holding
Tight, I say down girl, & she lies all cool
On the asphalt waiting to launch herself
At the next child in cleats, but only
With my say-so, & only to steal a kiss;
Shahid understands the desire to be seen
As more than a threat waiting to pounce,
& so instead of saying no baby,
I shout race, & we running these steps,
& my heart rattles & hers is audible,
Even as her paws turn Tay-Tay,
Two-steps at a time, & for a glimmer,
Into the DeLorean, & maybe I'm flying
Back, too, if to fly is to be unafraid
Of the sunrise in your rib cage.

Loss

& he said, we always laugh through loss,
As if that was the only way to construe loss.

When the dead have names we remember,
It is difficult to grasp this: a new loss.

Terrance Hayes's diction got beaucoup range;
Who knew? Our lives—not sadness, but a blue loss.

Affluence of pain—regrets of plethora—abundance,
Dear G–d, who will train us to do this? Consume loss.

Dear dead Black boy dying, we have all used you,
Taught to use your death to balloon loss.

When she was pregnant, under the moon—
That delightful fullness & how it confuses loss.

Not knowing the brother's name means nothing,
Being a fool ain't the blessing that excludes loss?

I tell my moms I'll divorce soon & she sighs.
Dear Juvie, tell me love ain't how we accrue loss?

In a fit of something, sadness or rage or was it desire?
Shahid began wearing the mask, to prune loss.

Rings

Everyone needs a reason to remember,
Even if remembering brings about tears.
Shahid will tell you he knows the ugliest among
Us gets ignored, remembers days he needed
To be a rugged child to disappear, &
Still failed to vanish, breaking bread with men
Who carried life sentences like clichés,
& so all these years later isn't surprised when
The smiling woman mentions Theo,
The mutt, half Chihuahua & half Puck,
So ugly that she is cute. What irony, the rescue
As plain as a pikestaff, huckory, no oil painting,
Is named G–d's gift. This is how love brings
You to tears. Some of us accumulate
Rings like dogs, each finger holding its own
Promise & history. Nugget, who takes permission
Without asking, standing on a coffee table
As if belonging, like five rings on this woman's
Middle finger, as brave as anyone, the rings
& coffee table saying: though she be small
She be mighty. Who adorns a single digit
With the beautiful part of brass knuckles?
Two empty fingers echo French bulldogs
Whose names I never learn. But this is how
Loss works. The losing itself is a naming,
& every story becomes multiplication,

If the naming is filled less with names than
With the best parts, the barking & everything
Else, because who among us hasn't been
As mangy as a rescue, even on our best
Days, desiring mostly to be loved.

Climbing Mt. Kilimanjaro

When someone dies on the mountain,
The terrain owns the body. Bones
Become ash & then landscape.
Every lover I touched has become
Part of the geography of my soul.
Sometimes, everything is a metaphor
For sex. This woman tells me you
Can't traverse the same path twice,
& I ask her to name what this is,
This woman who first saw me naked
Before hair covered our pubes
& now has seen the gray & trifling
Of a man who loves a woman
Who doesn't share his name. Tell
Me what ain't dangerous at 1am?
On a mountain, you don't look for
Guidance from Sirius, the North
Star or the galaxy of constellations.
The bones on the ground, brittle
Of leaf, the roaming animals,
Silence of the large stones all co-
Pilot or wait to stumble you into
Needing rescue. Some people
Are always done, or rather, finished,
Before the helicopter arrives;
Some people are the helicopter.
& again, I'm some fool laughing,
There are mountains, & there is
Knowing that second first time.

Lavaggio

These things we no longer do:
Ironing bills with our hands' ridge,
Hoping that when we slip the bill
Into the machine it releases coins
The way a payphone I'd shake
With both hands would do for me
At the Popeyes on the corner of Silver Hill
& Swann Rds. This Italian laundromat
Is so far from those streets. I remember
Around the way now, Saturday mornings
Washing clothes with my mother as a kind
Of wonder. We have not washed clothes
Together in more years than I remember,
& even remembering those years reminds
Me of how I loathed the detergent powder;
The tumbling of washers & dryers marking
Hours off like checkmarks on a jail calendar;
The large trash bags we carried nearly
A mile from our two-bedroom apartment.
I hated that we had no car, that my friends
Watched me troop with Moms as if our lives
Were in the things we carried. & Moms
Loves Italy & though she is not here with me
Today, on this trip where each day I return
To an Umbertide I pretend is home,
Despite not knowing enough Italian to order
A proper cappuccino before noon.
The German Shepherd & Poodle mix
I coo over on a friend's phone is another way

Distance teaches us love: how we remember
The barking things that transform us
Into something worthy of being protected.
The dog that has passed me is the same
Jack Russell Terrier I see each day,
With a patch of brown over his left eye
The little dog looks like the kindest pirate
On this planet. Of all the things I've plundered
To lose time. If only I could walk once more,
With a black trash bag larger than me,
To clean what playing outside left dirty.

Too Bad the Only
Suffering Ain't Weeping

for Alex

In a world where every touch hurts
Someone, the intimacy of a blade
Is worse, a kind of clarion & haunting
& who hasn't needed to be forgiven?
I was wailing in public is what I mean,
My right hand broken by believing
It could fly through a door, & the rest
Of me out of sorts from all that's been
Lost. Those understanding survival
As a last stand against the noose,
Wondered if we never or always get
What we deserve. Alelur means priest,
& who among us has not needed
A person close enough to violence
To rejoice at the ways mercy is often
Our only gift? It's like the robins, or
At least I want it to be like them, slow
Building a nest, a few twigs at a time,
Certain they'll sleep in the nesting box
They make, until they don't, & still
Being unbothered by how this work
Of twigs & straw makes them vulnerable
Enough to hesitate before flying from
Wooden fence to just behind the front
Bush. We're all hiding where everyone
Can see might be the point, & my
Broken hand was its own weeping
Way of asking a crowd of strangers
If I might be forgiven.

36 Empty Glasses of Wine

& a dog that appears as if an apparition,
But isn't that always the case in these
Chambers, where wild animals humor
Our need to be loved. Shahid spent
Years starving for love is what I fear
Confessing, as I wonder off alone,
& by the time I return, the table of 36
Glasses has become a symphony of wet
Fingers circling the rims of what has become,
As if by alchemy, musical instruments,
& then, without barking, the heart's echo
Returns & leaps into a lap at the closest table,
The quiet terrier just another curious diner.
& someone's little baby girl waves at me,
& Jamila, staring at the specially prepared
Vegan meal says, I wanna cry, which
Reminds us all how what brings you joy
Might bring you tears, as if or because your
Body is a flower starving for water.

Chrysanthemum

The blood came from the heart,
Nearly overwhelming the cavern
Holding it: Hemangiosarcoma,

A word to describe the leaving,
But never the populated years,
The nights when neighbors swear

They witnessed a coyote chased
By a wolf chased by a witch
(Only the coyote was real. You

Were the wolf; Lori the sorceress).
Nothing ever held you back
From returning, like your namesake,

Called, once, by Hawthorne, a flower
Of strange beauty blossoming in the wind.

Jethro's Corner

I Maps

The corner of Ashmun & York & the sometimes
When the only evidence is a map; the disappearing

English of old: *plat*, a funky word that exists most
In memory, meant *to make a plan or map of;*
To draw to scale; to plot.

A man who cannot read coordinates can still plot
On his freedom. Imagine a rectangle on the oldest
Map in these nine squares of geography

Once called a wilderness.

     Quinnipiac   Pequot   Paugussett

To plot freedom is to leave the words that matter
Written across everything you own that matters,
As in leave the names that your loves call you
All the places that you traverse.

As in, to name is to announce worthy of remembrance.

II Property

Some evidence of this life is always measured
By the weight of La Llorana's weeping.

Jethro Jethro Jethro Jethro Jethro
Jethro Jethro Jethro owed his name. Left
This world owed his name. Who enters heaven
Owed their name? Who enters nameless?

Historical Catalogue of the Members of the First Church of
Christ in New Haven, Connecticut A.D. 1639–1914
Compiled by Franklin Bowditch Dexter

CATALOGUE OF MEMBERS, 1726–28

May 15. **875.** Patience *Mix* (John) Alling   *May, 1786
             Daughter of Caleb and Mary (494); born March, 1699;
             wife of 1052.
        876. Mary *Atwater* (Isaac) Dickerman   *17—
             Daughter of 421 and 338; born Dec., 1686; wife of 605.
        877. Experience *Perkins* (David) Gilbert   *May, 1748
             Daughter of David and Deliverance (354); born Dec., 1699;
             wife of 1111.
        878. Jethro Luke (colored)   *1760–61

Franklin knew his name enough to count
Him more than 3/5ths,

To list his surname & call him colored,
To be counted & named, the fourth member
Whose lineage included a slave ship.

The first non-European with a surname listed,
An old English variant for happenstance,
For luck, which in the land of cotton is a variant

For the word irony, for deliverance, think Luke
Of the gospel, Luke the liberator, Luke as
English variant of Lucas, Lucius, bright, light

For a plot listed in the corner of a map.

Jethro Luke was colored, cast in shadows
Of manacles—or, in the parlance
Of Marx & Pareto: Jethro was owed,

Left owning little, beyond whatever he held
When his eyes searched the freedom of a night sky:

Brown coat ... old great Coat ... brown Jacket ... white Jacket,
1 check shirt ... black stocking ... old ax ... small tongs ...
old gun barrel ... great Bible ... 8 round bottles ... candle stick ...
old mare ... pair of oxen ... plow share

III Freedom
Is one way to name this story.
Sometimes only maps be evidence.
In 1748, a corner mark confesses:

Jethro a Black man farmer.

Jethro's Corner

Corner of Ashmun & York, a small city park
Cater-cornered to the Grove Street cemetery,
& all the freedom not permitted to rest there—

Jethro Ruth Mindwell Sampson Betty Joe
Jinny Mango Sanders Sabina Sibyl
Phyllis Dinah Pero Sume Pompey Gad
Rose Rhoda Phyllis Pompey Williams Newport
Amasa Silva Caesar Rose Cato Leah Socoro
Peter Alice Little George Jack York Pressey
Polly Caesar Peter Simeon Joseph Bristol
Nano Joe Jeff Congo Pomp Ben Cuff Phillis
Sharper Rogers Jack David Gardiner Dinah
Bet Alling Jack Geff Ruben Ruth Cambridge
Cuff Edwards Amy Belfast Fowler Primus
Tim Lenard Eli Harry Sue Daggett Gain Amey
Joe Place Jane Caesar Jin Daniel Thomas.

Bike Ride

for Micah

Returning from a gravel path,
I ride a bike with my oldest boy,
& this is where he learns how the body
Fails you. Each time I pause, he asks
If I'm okay, & I say yes & climb
Back on the bike as if I believe
I won't falter again. I know I will.
The ride no more than 2 miles
Along an Italian road but so much
More than my body can take these days.
We'd been searching for a haunted house
& I should admit that my son don't
Like birds, but when I'd found this
Abandoned church & hundreds of
Wings turned it into a scene from Hitchcock,
I wanted to share that mixture of joy
& fear I'd felt. I imagine he knew—
Mostly I wanted to be close to him
In a way that my father has never been
To me. Biking to that old church, we
Were interlopers, & discovered barking
That wanted us to take leave, particularly
The Gandolf looking like little mutt
In our path. Micah would have tangled
With the beast to save me, I know,
& as we ride, & I stop, & he asks
If I'm okay, I don't know what it means
For a child to see his father weep, but know
What it means to be saved by a son.

Roadkill

It's 3:41am & already I have biked the mile
From my first cell to the chow hall a half
Dozen times, if at all, & my body is tired enough,
& I admit to no longer wanting any of this.
The stars acknowledge no one at this time
Of betwixt & between & there is nobody to call,
& the dead black thing in the street is an animal
Until I get close enough to see that it's only
A bag flitting in the wind. We've all been mistaken
For something less alive in this life I know
As I stop my bike before a liquor store holding
Whiskey that no longer drowns me, & remember,
Standing beneath a flyer with a Black girl dancing
Under Basquiat's crown, forgetting who
Loves you is the easiest way to vanish.

Guns, dogs, & heroin

But not gin, not because of judgment
Or how some seduction reduces
Us all to a mistress of common sense,
But because the smell of gin ain't funky
Enough, not the guttural need that follows
Any get-down or birthday, you know, one
Of them walking in the rain-funky days,
Though not for the sadness but for the joy
Of more, & the cawing above says this world
Notices something other than me, & then boom,
I'm back on the Pettus Bridge, barefoot
In another downpour, on the other side a woman
I'd just met waits to return me to near
A memorial that stretches across so many acres
Of green, with its 800 giant Corten monuments
Falling from the sky, surnames, if known,
Of a Black person lynched in these
United States carved into steel, all for this
Legacy of survival we carry with our breadth,
& the two blue ribbons tatted behind this
Woman's ear, the J's with a dragon leaping from
The tongue on her arm, & her waiting as I walk
Quixotic across a bridge on a day that would-a-been
Rosa Parks 111th birthday, testify to all the ways
We come to know each other, & as I turn to see
The deadly, I stare down a fall that would foreshorten
The life of a falling g–d, & I remember Bloody Sunday,
How back then, even facing snarling, they'd held fast
To their Sunday mornings, & maybe this is what

The older couple remembers, the two I turn & see,
Walking just a pace behind what I've become:
A man barefoot & weeping in the rain, & they step
Without talking, but there, as if to tell me as I walk,
That today, a day of raindrops, augurs whatever men
Lost at sea desire when they fear drowning.

Guns, dogs, & heroin

In a Station of the Metro
(Don't You Remember)

Been running. Now buoyant.
This heart still a cauldron?
Love's truant: my voice hushed.
Tell me the g–d to pardon.

My heart? Still. A cauldron
On a train headed for trouble.
Tell me the g–d to pardon.
This falling ain't never been subtle.

On a train headed for trouble,
A red balisong on my mind.
This falling ain't never been subtle.
You remember our first time?

A red balisong on my mind,
That night, Luther's voice, & —
You remember that one time?
Running. Now. Buoyant.

We Never Say Goodbye

The silence of the night breathes
& this ain't the lonely of leaves raining
Onto a dark road after midnight;
& so one of us digresses
Us to a village in a country where
We've never held hands, where men
Transform silkworm cocoons into
Silk threads into quilts, the entire
Process alchemic, frayed remnants
Of a butterfly's past becoming
The quiet where lovers disappear
At night. Shahid knows that there
Is no disappearing in prison. What do
Any of us deserve? I close my eyes.
Touch a tooth mark beneath my heart.
Penitentiary cells nearly became my tomb.
I ducked contretemps & mischance.
What might I deserve? After
Some seasons, with this longing
Feeling like heroin? You. Breathing. Here.
& now, twice, my tears on your lips.

Tarragon

I touch teeth marks along my ribs
& my body becomes a tuning fork,
Again, humming as if you are here,
Your hands holding mine as if a man
Who is never safe is safe with you:
This memory, this hovering, a fucking
Impossibility in a world of almost.
You know how easily we might have
Missed this? Your body over mine,
My breath far more controlled
Than the beast inside me—that you
Call with your tongue? The scientific
Name for Tarragon is artemisia
Dracunculus, Latin for dragon g–ddess,
& I jy know the way my vulnerability
Becomes my heart's pleasure is delight
Only a dragon gives. & now you've turned
Me into a flame. What will I do?
Can a body whirr? Whistle? Caterwaul?
I've watched you simmer beneath me,
Beside me, while I lay above you,
My face lost in your paradise,
All your shuddering a yesterday or
Tomorrow I'll barter the off-kilter ruinous
Wild thing banging against your chest.
You hoard treasures because some
Searching lasts forever. Tell me I'm
The story you want to keep telling.
Tell me not to move. To relax. In

Eleven ancient texts, dracunculus
Is a symbol for healing; your skin
Juxtaposed with mine is my healing.
A shade before amber, some bronze,
Nipples of red dirt, a wonder of grays.
We are where flotsam finds home.
I touch a spot along my rib cage & feel
Your teeth against my flesh. Hold
My hands as the rattling inside me
Awakens & thrums. Once, I chipped
A tooth running it along the concrete
Of a mango. Let me run my teeth along
Your flesh, insatiable now as then,
Your river giving me this freedom.

What We Know

Just after the sun comes out,
Those with sleep still clinging
Slip into the street, before
Them two ears tilted toward
What the moon has said last.
Nose moving them from wonder
To the mission born of mystery;
Mystery moving them to mission,
From the wonder born of a nose.
This animal licks my face
With the same curiosity she uses
To pry what my youngest calls
A pigeon's treasure from the ground.
She shepherds me, just as around
Us, there are half a dozen others
Doing the guiding, animals
Who hear others call us & our
Jangle of inconsistencies, owners.
Before the sun has fully risen,
It's easy to see the truth of it all,
Those who would call me friend
But have never known soft paws
On their thighs would believe
That I am some lord, master, or
Minor g–d to this barking.
But I know I barely control
My wonder these days, & wish
To kneel & search with these
Dogs whose stance toward

Morning is so familiar, from sniffing
The air, to believing that even I,
A stranger, will turn & join, if
They bark in just the right way,
& then discover, once close
Enough to the looking, what has,
For whatever reason, become lost.

Bread Without Salt

There is always a price we aren't willing
To pay. & sometimes what we pay
Changes us forever. Saint Francis has his
Own story of prison. Near this rampart,
Along what was once a castle,
Capers burst through slivers & cracks
Because lizards eat the Flinders rose
& when they die inside walls where
Men have passed, flowers erupt from
Bellies, through layers of history & bricks.

Cascade

The sound is not rain,
But because it takes less
Time for the snow to melt
Than fall, from this wooden
Rocking chair small droplets
That were once snowflakes
Tumble to the unforgiving asphalt.
There is so much to say about
Things that are fleeting.
Once, I saw a small puppy
Run down my street after
Leaves drifting in the wind.
She could not name them leaves,
& probably was running after
The smell more than the wispy
Beauty. But ran she did, like
When my son looked into
The sky during his first snow
& said: mine, as a nearly
Imperceptible cold & delicious
Particle dropped into his hands.
Or it's like the boy in Italy,
& that trumpet of his. Of all
The people who stood around

Listening to those men
Blow their song into the cool,
Only he ran for the horn
He'd hope he'd need. Who
Cares about what songs
They played? All that matters
Is from inside some apartment
Or coffee shop or car on that
Street, the sounds were like
Sheets of rain, & of course
You'd step inside the cascade.

Running

The last time I ran with boots,
Officers would stop by my bunk
Afternoons when I was lucky,
& they would drop letters,
Always marked with the number
That defined me, back then
I would run with this Laotian
Cat & his stories of the home
He was exiled from, & it reminds
Me of how Red Onion State Prison
Won't let me go, & when we turn
Off this winding Italian road,
One I've biked at night, without
Lights or a helmet, & onto a trail
Unlike any prison's gravel, I wonder
If I've always chosen danger.
On the trail, barking dogs cheer
My body on, & there is Salome
& Res & Farah & Aart, & when
We see the pull-up bar, & I leap
To test my memory, this is almost
Like prison. I do ten. & as they
Count, I know as much as I am
Thinking of prison, I am thinking

Of how the desperation to survive
Turns what those around you say
Into the only gospel that matters,
& as I think of the stories I've told
In this Italian countryside, accompanied
By roosters & owls & birds chirping
That I cannot name, I hope that I've
Listened as well as I've spoken. All
There is in prison is listening, &
Maybe the stories are all a kind of
Chasing after a freedom that isn't
Dependent on the stories told,
But who dares listen.

Surrender

This is what Tay-Tay teaches me
One morning. I am walking her against
The wind, which means against everything
Holding me back, & it makes me pull,
Then yank her leash, when she urges us
Toward the street's opposite side, as if
She has not become one of my loves,
& most of the time she does obey
But on this morning she refuses
To relent & approaches the three-
Legged pit bull or bulldog or whatever
You imagine is fierce enough to destroy—
Even if that is me at sixteen with a pistol,
Is what I don't think, as Tay-Tay launches us
Toward the snarling & rampaging brown
Dog, that lies down as Taylor nears,
& reaches his tongue through steel bars
& licks my puppy's face, & Arthur, who uses
Three legs better than I've sometimes used
These two of mine, is said to just be lonely,
& to race up & down & bark with the only
Voice he has when possible friends pass,
& I'd been terribly afraid of the lonely
Barking, & Taylor's lesson is a gift,
The reminder of what it means to be
Generous, even when confronted with
What others (what we?) believe we need fear.

Solstice

Give me hunger. Fuck it. Your teeth
Against my neck. Give me tomorrows
& yesterdays. Tremble in my arms,
Scrape nails against my skin.
Give me trifling. Give me longing,
One more reason to return home.
Hold your breath. In Spanish the word
For love is the same as the word
For want. Tell me you have one more
Secret for me. You know how I came
To read my own palm? My calloused
Hands lifting this body up when
Hope was the memory of you. Days
When I pulled myself up from steel bars
Until my flesh rippled into the silhouette
Above your held breath. Your skin against
Mine. There is the thing that barking dogs
Do, & then there is us. Give me that.
One more time, before the river comes.

Burlesque

Incarnadine: carmine: cardinal.
You, a red balisong; your splayed
Hand on the chords of my belly. Wine
Colored: claret: burgundy: scarlet.
You cover my mouth with your lips
& I breathe you. Whisper to this stone
'Till it rattles like dice 'long my bones;
Your nails touch my knee. Your tongue:
Cerise: vermillion. My clarion call; antithesis
Of every brick, of every cell door. Florid:
Ruddy: hasper. A whisper. Maroon: rubicund.
I call your name. Rufescent: russet: copper.

This Morning

I've never had this kind of attention,
The way my puppy leans into
The dawn air knowing something
Is waiting, whether the squirrel she
Never catches or the birds or a leaf
Flying through the air like a tossed
Treat. There is so much of knowing
When to wait for the smell of the wind
To announce what to do that I've never
Understood. & this morning, when
My puppy, who is now older, but just
Barely, than my youngest was when he
Learned to climb a tree & notice when
I'm away, this puppy is more miles
From me than my sons have ever been,
& I wonder if today her nose, when
Turned to the wind, searches for me.

Will They Reminisce Over You

for Titus

Your father's name you've given back.
Nom d'artiste. When a name conjures
Waystations, all that's left is concoction,
The yarn, the half a dozen ways being
Present becomes the only promise,
Truly instinct: brain matter, diastole, systole,
Reflex action, the very first canvas.

San Giorgio

The mackerel rests on porcelain as if
It were a Piero fresco, some long-ago
Thing that has crystallized before me
By a magic I can name but not reproduce,
& still it reminds me of Sussex One
State Prison, of Tupac rapping about
Eating Jack Mack staring at these walls
In silence, though this too is about how
We find what we look for, & for all these
Years I've been looking for myself where I
Last knew me as not shaped by what fools
Name wisdom & my mother calls the reason
She weeps. What more of this world can anyone
Desire? Mt. Vesuvius is 4,589 miles from my
Mother's hometown & she once traveled there
To scale the 4,000-foot active volcano. As a
Child I was obsessed with Pompeii, with the idea
That mid-sentence you can become ensconced
In history, & I don't wonder when my mom
Says she would scale it all again. We have always
Been gamblers might be the point, never
Believed in quitting while we're ahead,
& since she once braved that history to grapple
With an old disaster, of course confronted with
Another, we'd go at it once more, because no one
Has ever asked, of Pompei, *were they beautiful*.

Exhibiting Forgiveness

I

for Miles

There are no lessons in jump shots.
The rackety clanking of the 26-ounce ball
In this gym that isn't home is just a cauldron.

My father has never seen me play ball
Is part of this. As if only a father's witnessing
Evidences your existence; existential,

If the only lesson of value is who shows up,
Even if with more things to be forgiven
Than time will number. My sons may never

Forgive me. My youngest slings jumper after
Jumper into a rim I couldn't reach with good knees.
There are always losses. It's always some father,

A son, doing the only needed thing after
A game of almost, & with every aching shot
His hands recall their skill & I want to say

That after all those parabolas, after
That night of restless sleep, after Miles, who
Has always been the most fierce on any

Court, suited up, again, in a city near Boston,
I want to say the seven straight buckets he made
Is what left hands wiping tears into a graying beard,

My face now my father's, & for a moment,
So early in the game the shot barely mattered,
As he watched that orange spherule slip

Through the nets like the hand
Of a pickpocket—I swear he turned my way,
As if to make sure I was witnessing it all,

The possibility of presence & tomorrow.

II
for Micah

To be free is to invent yourself —
Always, as if the dice you launch
Against the curb are loaded,

Certain to fall from your hands & reveal
Tomorrow's prophecy. We read
Our own palms: you the wonder,

Miracle & constellation, talisman;

Your silences, though like mine,
Are all your own— the turn of pages:
Gaiman, King, & NK Jemison;

Of bookmarks? For quitters, you remind—
Of jam spread across brioche;

Of all the ways that my regrets have become wings,

& everything that turns a man

Into a father. Maybe this is always the point:
You chase the asphalt of a track
& become everything I know of freedom,

Your arms launching you into every
Wild joy only a g–d would need name.

III

for Daven

Who admits it'll be this way?
A morning. Somehow, the small body
That once held your stillness is larger

Than everything in the world you notice,
& your father's shoulders or walk or voice
Become yours unexpectedly.

When every day is a change,
Your gift is still wanting to wrestle
An elephant, or finally outpace your father

In a footrace.

That afternoon you kept picking up
The basketball, & walking back to the same
Spot, jabbing with your right foot

& then launching towards the net,
Reminds me of Titus. It's the moment
Before, when you become your father

Paying attention, & then you're off,
As if no longer thinking, having decided.
& of course, this is the thing anyone wants,

Sons that will hold, even for a second,
In those moments before they leap
Into the disasters of the world,

Something of what we'd given them,
To carry them into those tomorrows with grace.

IV
for Savion

This is how they'll tell the story:
His father wrestled.

& maybe, in your head, you'll say
My father wrestled wild beasts, or my
Father wrestled with sorrow,

Or my father wrestled the world to become
The man who loves with joy

& not violence; & this is the story
That will matter more, as every moment
Becomes layered into what makes

The days make sense. These days, your father
Sends me photos of you & your brother
From those days when the space

You took up said nothing of the space
You'd come to hold, & I think
He means to say this is how

They'll know that a man
May have as many North Stars
In this world as he needs.

Grief

for Lori

The story of Easy, a small dog who
I imagine is named after Mosley's detective,
Crawls into the space left by Zinnia,
Burrowing into corners, against
Door frames, beneath a house —
In search of a phantom smell. State
Fair: Sahara: Thumbelina: Dreamland:
Envy. Orange Star. Creeping zinnias
That bloom until first frost. My g–d
The ways we grieve, again & again
Because the only rule of life
Is to forget means to abandon. When
I forget to feed Tay, she never barks,
But waits, wherever I am, as if she trusts
My memory more than I do. I imagine
This is grief's lesson: it is the engine
Of making what happened before
Matter, & it's true that I've only ever
Remembered a few joys as much
As I've recounted all my reasons
To grieve, but nothing grows
Without weeping, not even joy.

For Some Things There May Be Forgiveness Still

When my mother asks
After my heart, she senses
More than knows this weeping,
& call it coincidence, or maybe,
Finally, an admission: years
Lost to prison; no, years lost
Because I pulled a pistol
On strangers, became
A chasm we might tumble
Into & then she stumbles
Again, watching me occupy
Space for more days since
Back when I was her teenager,
As if I vanished & never
Returned. & now my sons
Approach my disappearing
Age. & I wonder what to name
This thing that's held us
Together all these years.
Maybe it is like crows & how
They've turned murder into
Paradox, a way to announce
Never being alone, such wild
Juxtaposition, hundreds
Of cawing black birds
Named after death testifying
To life, in wild & raucous flight.

Arriving Late

The only one on time was the dachshund,
Doing what Richard Pryor would have called
Low-running, away from the airplane that felt
Like a cage to him. Shahid has known prison
Cells to feel like a cage & has remembered
His name in returning to what the small dog
Would escape. The sniffing dachshund became
A reminder that sometimes freedom means
Noticing what others miss. My mother
Stood beside me, & we were at an airport
The day before Mother's Day. G–d knows
The second Sundays of May I've spent
In cells, & I should have known being with
Her on this one was all the joy I needed.
Our missed flight had become a chance
To lose ourselves in the despair of missed
Connections & layovers. Elsbirth, behind
This ticket counter but from an island
As lovely as my mother, said, *I would*
Have saved you two that missed
Flight. But then what of the moments
That followed? When my mother saw me
In public dancing with strangers, if to dance
Is to test out words. In an Algerian dialect,
Dsara means, roughly, trying hard to befriend
A stranger with words, & this is why
I confess to the bartender: my ring finger,
Now as barren as a prison cell when I left
It for good. My g–d the prayers answered

By leaving. May g–d forgive us for not
Knowing that we have always been enough,
For ourselves, & definitely for the small
Dogs, who appreciate the chance silence
Gives to notice what's been missed.

Daffodils

When every fancy is freedom,
Hunger becomes discovery—hold me
That way again, your hand gripping
One of the blades you love, my body
All tremble & want. Sometimes
Surrender is the only gift. My hand
Returns to a space beneath my heart,
& I feel that raucous ragtime moon
Song beating against my chest. Can,
You hear this when I'm hovering?
That day, riding down a stretch
Of highway that led to my prisons,
The daffodils had no business blooming
Then, in that March 4th frost, in the same
Way we had no business becoming,
But these yesterdays precede us,
& I wonder where won't you follow.
So, we chase down my past as if
There is freedom in the cells I left
Behind, & you will tell me that inside
I am in my element, which means I
Shimmer, as if a man can rise from
A corpse & walk into the world. I was
A corpse before you touched me is
What I'm thinking, as I resist asking
You to pull over, stopping to pluck
A half a dozen daffodils & thread
The lot of them into your hair.

The Things We Carry

The collie is part of the story,
The DJ, the warm rum
We sip as the room fills with
Familiar sounds, then memory,
Then ache. Imagine—the musical
Lexicon in this Italian bar familiar
As a game of spades. & few
Speak English, but when DJ spins
The Rhythm of the Night, I think
Of the King biography in my knapsack,
& the losses needed to get us peace,
& then a child tosses an orange globe
To her sister, & I think *pallacanestro*,
The Italian word for basketball I
Learn because of Kobe, & we toast
In Creole, English, & Spanish, languages
We've left to get here, communing over
Tobacco & rum. & we tell each other
The stories of the lands that birthed us
& the troubles we harbor, & tonight when
The lights go down & I get up to dance
A dance I've not danced since I last
Thought of Michael K. Williams, the other
Dancers don't watch me. When the drum

Solo begins, the man with the 80s
Are Back T-shirt spins around with a baby,
& my crush, with her flash of white hair
& lit cigarette, pulls a smiling woman
Into this growing circle, & they all
Pirouette around me, even the collie,
& despite the ways we've suffered,
This dancing says: we've learned broken
Is more waystation than destination.

That's the Sound

for Winfred Rembert

I

The light cast under a fedora:
Memory of the South's desperation
Of woe: sweatbox, noose, poplar;

History etches into this
Brother's watery eyes, my G–d
Must we always suffer tears.

They just wanted to be cruel to you.
I had been through so much in my life before
I went to the chain gang.

II

It is always so much, always the same crown
Of tears, the reason why the yoke pulls
You back again & again to the wrong yesterday.

What does the tapping against leather
Tell the woman you love?

The tapping of leatherwork

Not much hope in it
Since everything is done from the past

III

Somebody's after me
Ands I don't know what to do

Talking about the past & I remember
This story my father tells me once
About how he had put a gunmetal .45

Next to two fingers of Hennessy, turned
The barrel until it is a muzzle against
His sternum & told me to pull the trigger.

All with a straight face, as if it had happened,
Told me three times, as if I'd betrayed a G–d.

I think I'll go on home to grace
With what I've got holding me down
Holding me back

IV

Always something holding you back.
The bullshit is that the albatross
Is a sign of hope & not something
Around your neck.

The stories belong to all of us,
Paints this man who pulled himself
From the landscape of lost.

In the sweatbox, your mind is talking
To you constantly. I'm thinking, Am I going
To really lose it? Am I broken?

V

Turn the down down down down sorrow
Into something that feel less lonely,
Suffering in art feels like somebody made
It to tomorrow, at least, baby, tell me that's true.

Moving Fast Backwards

For those of us mad about the ways Black men
Get sainted, with death & scorn, with prophecies
That doom their children, there is Bobby Jones,
Who walked like a man who knew he was beautiful,
Who would crack a bottle against a curb
Before launching himself into the air
At what others would say was a man's jugular
& he might admit was a destiny he sought to avoid,
All the disasters that happen when violence
Isn't enough to save you. Doesn't sainthood begin
With not being saved by another? For those of us
Maddened by the inability to remember being
Held by someone who loved us more than whatever
Holds them down, there is the story of handwritten
Letters from a cell in the County, & how euphemisms
For prison: the Bing, the Clink, Lockup, the Last Stop,
The Big House, & all, turn geography into prophecies
That men doomed struggle to avoid—ain't no telling
All that Shahid avoids to sing this song, as if long
Ago someone said you get to choose: be a witness
Or a saint, & the boy who was still just a boy knew
That witnesses live whereas saints become the bread
Of other's nurturing. & the living ain't easy. A violence
Ran through Bobby Jones's veins, the man swore his life
Was pulled from the lines of an Iceberg Slim tale,
& maybe it wasn't violence, as much as thirst,
The kind of thing that makes a brother add ketchup
To his eggs, as if to say seeing red can sometimes
Mean possibility, like holding a woman on some night

That ended up being enough, & having her remember
That you can sing, even if you can't, even if the only
Song of that night was moaning, loving a woman so good
That everyone forgets the definition of sainthood
Is to move backwards fast, to always be lost retracing
Your steps. He even named the German Shepherd
Lady, as if part of commitment is calling it like you see it.
There is a whorehouse somewhere & that is likely
Where Bobby was transformed from witness
Into the man who would pummel a friend that confessed
To wanting a piece of his daughter, the child
Others would say smelled like him when anger welled
Up into some wild river & she remembered that being
Beautiful ain't never saved nobody, not Bobby Jones
Of whom a friend once confessed, I knew your dad,
That was one pretty nigga that could rhyme. & he said
It smiling, as if he imagined being the man's lover,
Which is just to say that there are men so beautiful
That everything they do provokes desire.
He'd cross His legs like a beautiful woman after a long day &
Never feel threatened, because saints know
That there is so much more to weigh you down
Than being comfortable. Maybe the word never saves.
Nor smack, horse, junk, skag, shit, brown & everything
Else men turn into the bricks they use to accumulate
All the money that drowns them, before that narcotic
Becomes the thing that keeps them from knowing
To fly you have to let go of all the shit that weighs
You down. It's hard to let things go, that's how

It is with them all, men destined to become those
Whose memory saves us more than their lives.
Bobby Jones was a palace with a city rising out of him
Is what his friend said, the man he pummeled for reckless
Eyeballing his baby girl, the first thing Bobby knew
He had to protect. & like all saints, he lived as if he knew,
Everything is art, if you try hard enough.

Otherwise

The crescendo of barking is this Italian countryside's chorus,
These yelping hounds, scattered in homes like men Shahid
Knows—spread among cells in prisons, in slave & free
State alike, & the yelping call to each other as if echolocation
Is all you need to enjoy what makes them sing, & I am cycling
Amid the serenade, this bike how I eclipse the miles
Saint Julian walked as I return to a café in Umbertide without
Knowing if the story the barkers tell is of the stranger banking
These sharp turns with forgiveness as his only light.

Of All This

& it all reminds me of the small dog that walks with me,
Mostly barking, & of days I'd drive her to happy homes,
Where she'd board & riot with the local cacaphony, & it reminds
Me of how, as we'd pull up, before the car full stopped, she'd be
On two paws, full leaning her mouth against the glass as she
Shouted her joy & maybe I shouldn't be surprised when she
Bounds from my car & barely pauses before launching herself
& me toward the green door from behind which those who
Have become her pack wait. But I am always surprised,
& astonished, too, that she can leap into my arms & leap away
& have entirely no clue how sometimes you want, in a way
That's familiar from one continent to another, to the fowl
& wind & flowers & even the gravel that people carrying
A stone in their heart have walked on, that feeling, for
A moment, for at least a second, if that, to just fucking howl.

Apologia to the Stag

after Piero della Francesca's fresco of Saint Julian

Because, maybe, there was no stag
& the only curse was anger.
Blame desire—to desecrate, destroy,
Turn from prayer. What if Julian knew,
As we all know, when we test disaster,
& venture toward the last ledge,
Some lonely cherubim pulling
Us back, except we don't breathe
& instead shatter our histories;
What if there were no stag & only
The pause after, where escaping
Yesterday becomes folly
& recovery demands invention—
Shahid has lived in cities of men
Who know what it means to fail
To turn away. A man can walk
Until all his steps become sorrow,
& maybe others will name it pilgrimage,
& over two fingers of rum, maybe
They'll tell this story of the stag
Whose warning was ignored, & they
Will never say it was a collie or hound
Or small terrier that barked no,
Because then we'd know the lie

Of warning, know that a dog would
Leap before a blade to save the last
Bit of goodness we have, & so it is
A stag we hear of, instead of the horror
Of a man who should have paused.
& haven't we all been that man? Imagining
We might have listened if the voice
Warning was more eloquent or a bark
Or at least the stag we wish warned
Him? They say, the woman who took
His hand knew him better than the blood
That covered them, & years later, no one
Will say she was wrong, even then,
Knowing that when they left that disaster,
He was hoping to assemble what he'd broken,
The very best way he knew.

Arches

Nothing but sand, silica & oxygen,
& all the possibilities that come from
Distributing weight that would crush
You to where it would save. & it is all
So boring to the labrador, who desires
No more than to turn all the world
Into a spectacle to be smelled. In Rome,
There is a building with 80 open
Doorways. So much possibility; such
Homage to death. The Latin for
Sand is arena. At the Colosseum, so
Much possibility; such homage to death.
The dead & soon to be emerged from
Beneath the ground. My dog sniffs
Wherever she is, as if wondering or
Searching or remembering the men
& women & children & animals buried,
Waiting to emerge, as some spectacle
For us, some new death she, the littlest
Dog I know, might save them from.

Will She Think This Makes Me Good

There is a road that stretches from one part
Of town to another, & one morning, walking
That asphalt, away from or toward my troubles,
I saw a barking dog ready to cross traffic,
& forget what I thought as I mad-dashed
Into the rush of caffeinated sedans yelling
no no stop hold up stop stop, outstretched
Arms as if desires matter when confronting
Some disasters, as if anyone's desires matter
Faced with cars just barely beyond screeching
& this dog close enough to know she would kill
Us both if she ran toward me as if I were
Her savior. My life had just become a tender thing
In this quiet dark-eyed animal's small jaws,
No longer barking, astonished at what she
Had to know was not my sacrifice, but my need,
To tumble into this unforgiving life hoping to save
One living thing other than myself—I never tell
People of all the times I've done nothing, failed
To answer the call or pour something into
The starving cup asking for change
Or run back towards the danger, though
I once admitted to knowing twice being scared
Should have mattered less, the second time
When T stopped eating, the sobbing dog behind
Me sounding too much like any abused
Animal to be ignored, even by me, who ate
Cantaloupe covered by a different dead animal,
& couldn't hear the abuse for a desire not to

Witness one more broken thing, & such is this
Life, where not looking then now has made
A friend of this no longer rattled small dog
Named, I'd later learn from the man who
Belongs to him, Porkpie, after the hat jazzmen
Wore as they invented new ways to wonder
Will this woman think this makes me good?

A Chaos of Welcome

This dog bends toward the ground
With everything, a tipped nose,
Bent knees, strained shoulders leaning
Into whatever smell beckons, straining
Against the leash & if there is one,
G–d. I know the feeling. Mornings
Walking a puppy that looks enough
Like this one, makes me almost stop
My bike on this Italian road at 6am,
To share a photo of Tay. This Italian
Meanders down this quiet street,
The Jack Russell desiring little more
Than to be prostrate with her desires.
To be prostrate is to show reverence.
I've seen men bend their bodies toward
The ground in prayer & in drunkenness;
I've been a man weeping into his own
Welcoming hands, my body shaking
As if weeping is ablution, reverence,
Submission. We should stop, sometimes,
& tell a stranger or try to confess,
Even if he doesn't share our language,
That on this morning you see him
As you've been, holding a small dog
That is the only beating heart holding
You to the ground, even as all she
Wants is get closer to the things
Worshipped, all the while wondering
What keeps you from doing the same.

Caffe Saccari

Simone walks up to me & this place
Becomes another kind of home.
How to admit this? In every city I love
I've been a stranger. How to say I love
How on my walk here, I wait for Lassie,
Two of them, white & eager to bark
As I pass their home? I have become
Someone who welcomes the loud bark
Of a dog that would have frightened
Me late into my thirties. Taz may be the
Same breed as the pair that says hello,
& I know he is large enough to tumble
Me to the ground in play, & am still unafraid,
Even if I'd be surprised, just as now, when
The Italian who offered me a ride on a lonely
Night, when three of us, with languages
Bridging colonialism, were stranded
In this strange city, calls out Reginald
As he approaches this café I've sat at four
Consecutive days, & realize in every place
I've known I've collected names as souvenirs:
Shahid, Reggie, Young Music, Jojo Santana,
All a way for people to do as Simone
Does now, offer me welcome, as a way to say
Kindness makes us no longer strangers,
& then he offers to show me his city,
Where I will be a stranger, still, but less so,
Because of friendship he extends to a man
Who has only now learned to weep.

Canary

Sitting still, on a street with a name
I cannot recall, is a Coupe de Ville.
I always wanted to sing, seduce
A crowd with the terrible in my voice,
& mornings, driving by this song
Of my past, often I slow as if to see
Is to climb behind the wheel & return
To the moment that could have
Changed it all. I sweated that ride
Like I worried over finding my falsetto,
Even after Amaud let me know to reach
Those notes—*a man essentially cuts
His own throat*. Something about desire
Frightens me. I started to love that canary
Spaceship & then discovered de ville
Is a French word for town hall:
Maybe some don't need an audience.
I didn't expect to land here, where
I tell you there is no city for me
To claim, admit I've learned to belong
In what meaning comes from this
Cadillac that never moves, but reminds
Me of times when all my baggage
Was expectation. A lover once showed
Me how everyone deserves to expect
Tenderness. & I drive by that version
Of my yesterdays & know that there is
Always something to cherish so much
It makes you sigh, as some longing might.

Memorial Hoops

The late May day broke a record for cold,
For us wanting to be anywhere but outside,
& it was the weekend we call Memorial.
My mother shipped off to the Iraq War a day
After her fiftieth birthday, but that is a story
For another time. We were driving into
The mother of rivers state: my youngest,
Named after a man who turned a trumpet
Into a riot, me, & friends who also believed
Watching their sons trade baskets with strangers
Was a kind of holy. Around us was more granite
Than Black folks & I carried Primo Levi's *If
This Is a Man* in my knapsack, hesitant to return
To all the astonishing ways we make each other
Suffer &, still, somehow, survive, & astonished
By how we remember. I've forgotten my share
Of things that matter. But who am I kidding?
The weekend was about basketball. We'd driven
Three hours to this colder weather. My youngest
Hoped he'd heat up once a ball graced his hands.
These were the days when he & the nine he suited
Up with desired little more than to hear the rasp
Of a ball against whatever passed for wood
In a gym with a hoop. There is something about

How basketball makes men of boys & boys
Of men. The other team had a player who made
Me think, though she be but little she is fierce,
As she, the only girl on the court, slipped a jewel
Into that hovering crown we cheered, even we
Whose boys sought to dribble & jump shot
Their way to the glory of a win. & when Miles
Came down as if he knew, I didn't hold my
Breath: a crossover, the ball then swung around
His back, the kid before him lost on some raft
In a wild river. Maybe Miles knew the ball would
Fall true, because he turned to watch us as much
As to get back on defense. & we laughed & laughed
& laughed as kids barely large enough to launch
All that need at a target did so, again & again.

White Peonies

This is how it happens, one morning
The ground is only the ground, & then
Green shoots through the rich brown loam.
I learned the word loam when I was starving
For something: fools would call it love,
& I would say it was a time machine, longing
For some days, months, years, when the sorrows
Didn't bloom like this thing from the ground
That I can barely name. Tell me how these
Peonies have migrated from Asia to my garden,
Have found their way into my line of vision
Despite prison & all the suffering I don't speak.
It all happens so sudden is what I mean to say,
When sadness becomes a beauty before your
Eyes so startling you ask friends what to name
The flower before you. I admit, I've pretended
To be g–d. To give a name to this thing that gives
Me joy. I called it Sunday, & then called it
After my firstborn. Have you ever been so rattled
By the unexpected that you wanted someone's
Blessing to name the thing? The peonies are so
Lovely they frighten me. They grow on thin stems
Longer than my arms with blooms heavier
Than the stalks. But isn't it always so? The beauty
Of the world so hefty we fear the world
Cannot stand it? & yet, why would we not want
To pray when we notice? Why do we forget that
Naming is the first kind of prayer, even as the white
Flowers turn into scented oil against my skin.

Balisong

for Can

This knife's duet is the only blues
I listen for some days, the song I hear
When the talon you pull turns blue
Against my skin's burnt umber. Prison blues?
A geography of losses. But your scent,
Your skin is my way-back-when kind of blue.
Imagine being the storm & what it blew.
I'll suffer for this. Who don't need this song?
So desperate for something, a song
Not tied to whatever is the blues
Of the prisons I've known. But I digress. I'll
Love you, is that what I'm saying? This isle,

Once some fool's fantasy, now our isle?
Where a man can traverse the blue
Vows of a song? Call out my name & I'll
Keep you in this wretched mind of mine; I'll
Keep you in whatever place I call here,
As in home, a teddy-bear in your arms. I'll
Be the talons in your hands; be the isle.
Touch yourself as if no one watches. Blues?
My smiles now windchimes in a storm. Blue?
Not this 4am shivering sky witness as I'll
Be pitching early morning woo. This song
Is a knife against my flesh, the song

Of a man who hustled for this, the song
Of a man traversing barefoot on an isle.
Our mothers' sorrows ain't our song;
Your eyes' chiaroscuro is our song.
& I admit to desiring it all, the blue
Of the softest place on earth, that song
From you, called with my tongue, the song
Of a dinghy pulled to shore, pulled here,
By the strength left in these arms, you hear
Me singing to you, my entire body the song
You call to being in this world. This scent
I've known. Teach me to relax. Who sent

Shahid to reremember himself in the scent
Of a river: solstice, tarragon, balisong
For a man whose life is a tightrope. You sent
Gifts of knives, four-leaf clovers, the scent
That comes when we turn a bed into an isle.
We found sea lions before a storm. You sent
Me a note with a secret. My two cents?
You're free as a sharpened blade. You read blue
Clouds, the moon, dirt, gravel, & the blues
Of my sorrow turn this blade that I've sent
You into a promise, the why of the river here.
For this? On any night, if we listen, we hear

My heart become the rapids you adore. Here,
Where you hold me with your thunder. Blues?
This is all the song I need. This here
Is the kind of thing I'd welcome ruin for. Here,
Where ribs meet my chest, your bite a song
I crave. This ain't madness. I can hear
How my heart becomes a song for you here,
When I am home, when I am yours. I'll
Be your dinghy, meet you on an isle,
Home is wherever we become us. Here
We are whatever joy turns a knife's blade blue,
All of it, every way these solstice blues

Gave us these blue flames. You salved my blues,
Making it easy like Sunday morning. Here
Is always a song. Say you love where this sent
Us. I keep saying song when I mean forever.
I keep saying forever when I mean Love. I'll. Isle.

Acknowledgments

Because I can. Back in the day, back in the '80s, in PG County, MD—a small enclave bordering this nation's capital—those three words served answer & exclamation. Coming up, if somebody asked, *Why you do that?* & you could say, smooth as someone not trying to be cool, *Because I can*—whether shouted or whispered under your breath, it meant that you believed you had business doing the thing done. & bet this, let that thing be executing a pirouetting up & under lay-up, snagging a one-handed grab of the pigskin, saying something something to whoever you imagine might be a tenderoni, or dropping a finished & aced test on a teacher's desk before anyone else—the feeling of having done a thing was the same. Truth be told, the shouting was meant to announce audacity more than strength—*because I can* was a way to confess that you believed you could do the thing, even if no one else did.

    Doggerel takes me back to a feeling that I first discovered in prison. When the central thing I believed in was that poetry matters. This collection starts with poems written when I was a teenager in Red Onion State Prison, a super maximum-security penitentiary in Virginia. & back then, I'd read my poems to the men in solitary cells around me, men who were strangers other than our shared prison. & back then, the poems mattered, if at all, because I read them aloud.

    These days, & with the poems in this collection, I found myself writing to read to strangers & I have read every one of these poems to a stranger, some-where, & the doing of that has reminded me of what it means to be a poet, which is to say, reading to strangers reminded me that my poems always have an audience & my quest, as it were, is to find a way to pay attention to the audience, even when I cannot name them or their geography or their sorrows or joys.

& so, let me thank the many ears who lent me a minute to sing. The woman who let me bor-row that umbrella in Montgomery, Alabama. She listened to "Balisong," then sighed in the way that women do sometimes. *Brother, you can keep that umbrella*. & the Uber driver, the nice young woman who listened to me read a poem about losing weight while she drove us to the Edmund Pettus Bridge for me to walk across barefoot in the rain. I owed you a poem—I hope you read my riff on dogs & the blue ribbons tatted behind your ear. & to the man in my apartment building, who I read "Running" one early morning, mak-ing the dog whose name I cannot remember wait another moment before smelling the morning grass. He said I have a beautiful voice & a beautiful beard, but he said nothing of the poem. His dog barked though. & the priest that I read the poem about Saint Julian & the nun, who two or seven days before I read the same poem. For the young man whose day of working the museum counter was interrupted by a poem. For my Uber driver that morning in Mississippi, who I read a poem about a man & prison & a dog & who'd go on to introduce me to the music of Jelly Roll.

Let me thank Granny 100. I was with a friend
headed to a prison to read poems to men I once served
time with & we stopped to visit her 102-year-old
grandmother & she told Granny 100 that I'd write
a poem on the spot if she just uttered a subject. &
Granny 100 said Sweet Jesus & I sang about the short-
est verse in the Bible I know: Jesus wept. Because
haven't we all wept? & doesn't the singing sometimes
make the weeping more than just sorrow?

&, of course, I want to thank the specific people
who made this possible. For James. We been work-
ing together on books now for long enough for me to
know if we ain't doing the marauding at midnight,
we ain't being alchemic. & to Lawanna, who said the
thing I needed to hear when I was reeling in Jackson,
Mississippi that night. But let me say this one thing.
Back back back in the day I picked up an issue of
Callaloo, a literary journal long edited by Charles
Rowell. I was in prison then, reading poems to learn
how to write them. The table of contents of that issue
listed a poet with the name DJ Renegade, & the very
idea that an esteemed journal would publish a cat
named Renegade made me believe poetry was a world
where your poems mattered as much as anything
else. That poem, "El Magnifico," was about Roberto
Clemente, & what astonished me when I'd meet DJ
Renegade (formally known as Joel Dias-Porter) years
later was learning that he was Cape Verdean & not
from the Puerto Rico that Clemente called home, &
still in the poem, Joel talks about Clemente as a father
figure, talks about weeping at the death of a man
he'd never met. Crazy, but of the layering of things
that made this book happen, the most important

was being reminded that for a poet, the heart more than anything else should drive what's written.

Anyway, Renegade came to New Haven & over two days we went over every syllable in this book. & it reminded me of when poetry meant chopping it up with friends on how to make words make sense. & so, the list of those who read these poems or listened to them, friends who are brilliant artists & writers & regular folks is too long to name, but I should offer one name here: this doesn't get done without the homie Lori Gruen. It's not even that she read every poem in here or listened to it countless times, but when I was in the deepest darkest depression of my life & feeling more alone than anyone should have to feel, Lori talked to me every single day, abiding tears, anger, silence with the kind of care & generosity everyone deserves.

Truth be told, my sons, Micah & Miles, have always been my muses. & these poems, where I found myself unwittingly trying to capture some joy, found me returning constantly to them. How do you thank your children for helping you understand what might be possible?

& of course, this book was inspired by the dogs who've welcomed me into their lives, from Taylor, our Jack Russell Terrier, to Zinnie, to Alec, to Hugo, to the dog who posed with *Redaction* after I'd run into her & her friends at the top of East Rock. But mostly, to the discovery of a world of friends, who walk on four feet, & including Feisty, the cat, a rescue, that circles my legs whenever I sit near her, & purrs that doggerel is kind of incomplete without a cat.

Reginald, a
somewhat
complicated man
prematurely set
in his ways,
decided at sixteen
to leave home.

Traveled many
miles to get to
prison and meet
young men turned
old, flying backwards...

- experience was
a cold teacher
nurturing
a rebelliousness
that dared to wander,
dared to achieve.

He left prison
a couple
of years ago,
I hear
he's making out
okay.

4'99

town and sanctuaries
refuse to cover our backs.

A statue
Sangha

assata 11.00
push

john edgar wideman
Maximus loosing a priest 10.95
middle passage 19.95

john edgar
14.95

Joyce
Johnson

4/0 383 2004
4/0 728-0877